AURORA

A PHOTOGRAPHIC JOURNEY

AURORA

A PHOTOGRAPHIC JOURNEY

CHRIS FRAME AND RACHELLE CROSS

WITH A CAPTAIN'S PERSPECTIVE FROM CAPTAIN WESLEY DUNLOP

The
History
Press

For Zac, Callum and Madeline

First published 2018

The History Press
The Mill
Brimscombe Port
Stroud
Gloucestershire
GL5 2QG
www.thehistorypress.co.uk

British Library Cataloguing in Publication Data.
A catalogue record for this book is available from the British
Library.

ISBN 978 0 7509 8582 6
Typesetting and origination by The History Press
Printed and bound in India by Thomson Press India Ltd

CONTENTS

ACKNOWLEDGEMENTS

We wish to express our thanks to everyone who has helped and encouraged us to share the *Aurora*'s photographic journey.

Special mentions go to:

Captain Wesley Dunlop, for your company aboard the ship and your help in answering many questions about the ship and her operations; as well as your friendship.

Rob Henderson, P&O Historian, for writing the foreword and providing photographic assistance; and to you and Doug for your ongoing friendship.

Jenny Hedley from P&O Cruises Public Relations Team for assisting us aboard, as well as Michael Mullane, *Aurora* Entertainment Director, for the fabulous tour of *Aurora* and your encouragement and support of our maritime lectures while aboard.

Amy Rigg, Alex Waite, Glad Stockdale, Martin Latham, Lauren Newby and Helen Bradbury, as well as the whole team from The History Press for your support and encouragement over the past decade. This book is released on the 10th anniversary of our first book published with The History Press. To have had a stable and supportive team for a decade has helped make each book possible.

Wesley Dunlop, Patricia Dempsey, John Frame, Rob Henderson and Andrew Sassoli-Walker for your photographic assistance, and our families for supporting us.

All images unless otherwise acknowledged were taken by Chris Frame or Rachelle Cross.

FOREWORD ❍ by Rob Henderson
P&O HISTORIAN

For over 60 years I have been associated with the sea and ships, mostly P&O group ships. My father, who was one of those legendary dour Glasgow engineers, once told me that the two most perfect man-made structures were ships and bridges.

Well, I don't know much about bridges but I do agree with him that ships will talk to you. Many years later I mentioned this to an old salty dog, a retired ship's captain whom I often met for a chat over a pot of tea.

'Ah yes,' he said, 'they talk all right. Walk her decks, feel the beat of her engines beneath your feet, listen to the sound of her movement and her partnership with the sea.

'Observe her design, the flow of her lines, when you stroll her lounges do you feel free and at ease, comfortable is the word, welcomed by the crew, embracing and secure. It might start at the top, the lower decks or in the centre, but if the crew appreciate that very special quality called the soul of a ship then it really will talk to you.'

Aurora is such a ship, a very special ship with a very special soul and in the hands of Rachelle and Chris this book will bring *Aurora* to life for you to enjoy and hopefully experience for yourself.

Top: *Aurora* in Sydney following the addition of the Union flag to her bow. *Above*: When *Aurora* came into service she had a white hull and buff coloured funnels. Courtesy Patricia Dempsey.

INTRODUCTION

P&O Cruises has a long and rich history. The line was established in 1823 as Wilcox and Anderson Co., a partnership between Brodie McGhie Wilcox and Arthur Anderson.

The fledgling company originally offered packet (sail) cargo transport to the Iberian Peninsula, with some passenger accommodation available. In 1830 the line began to invest in steam technology and in 1835 the company was renamed the Peninsular Steam Navigation Company to reflect the adoption of this technology.

In 1840 a Royal Charter officially incorporated the company; it was at this time that the line became known as the Peninsular and Oriental Steam Navigation Company, with Oriental added to the name in anticipation for an expansion into the Far East.

P&O's early years operating primarily between Britain and the Iberian Peninsula left their mark on the company, with the colours of the P&O flag being taken from the Spanish and Portuguese flags.

P&O is often credited with inventing cruising, an accolade that dates back to the early days of Arthur Anderson. An entrepreneur, the then newspaper executive placed an advertisement in the *Shetland Journal* describing a pleasure voyage by sea. Though imaginary, it created a great deal of interest.

Having successfully pioneered cruise-like voyages (known as the Grand Tour), P&O gained further notoriety as operators of pleasure voyages during the lean years of the Great Depression when they sent a number of their liners cruising.

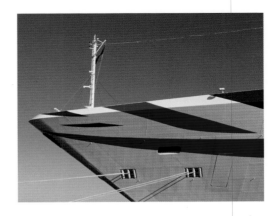

Top and *above*: *Aurora*'s bow displays the revised livery of P&O Cruises UK.

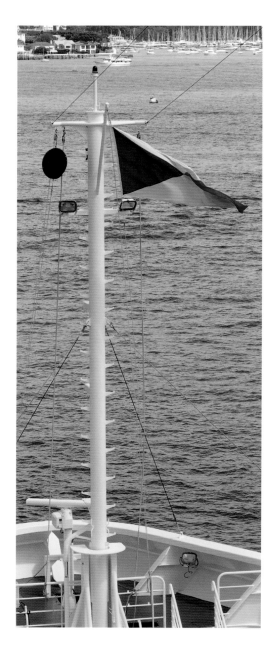

P&O Cruises still utilise the traditional P&O house flag.

The growing demand for cruising was in part due to the affordability of this style of holiday – which is still true of cruising today.

In 1961 P&O formally merged with the Orient Line to form P&O-Orient. At the time of the merger, the 41,910-ton liner *Oriana* was the most iconic vessel in the Orient Line fleet, while the 45,733-ton *Canberra* was the P&O equivalent.

Oriana was paired with *Canberra* and together the two ships helped the line transition from traditional ocean liner voyages to full-time cruising.

A generation later a new *Oriana* was built. Entering service in 1995 she was briefly paired with *Canberra* before the elder P&O liner's retirement. The success of *Oriana* led to Project Capricorn, a design for a larger running mate.

This ship became *Aurora*, her name taken from the archives of the Orient Line.

Aurora was built for the British arm of P&O Cruises at the Meyer Werft shipyard in Papenburg, Germany. She entered service in April 2000, and was launched by HRH The Princess Royal.

Today P&O Cruises is part of the Carnival Corporation and operates two distinct fleets of passenger ships.

Their luxury brand, based in Britain, is easily distinguished by the large Union Flag painted on the bow of the ship and their blue funnels sporting the line's emblem in gold. P&O Cruises' Australian arm operates a smaller fleet of ships and offers a more casual cruising experience.

Aurora has proved to be a very popular ship, offering family-friendly cruises and regular world voyages. Her facilities and her ambiance draw many passengers back for return sailings.

Aurora was refurbished in 2014 and was the first ship in the P&O fleet to receive the new hull art. The 2014 refit also addressed the ongoing mechanical issues which had plagued her early career.

Today *Aurora* is a welcoming home away from home for her guests, and a great way to see the world.

Aurora has a terraced stern and a much longer bow than many modern cruise ships. Courtesy Patricia Dempsey.

WELCOME ABOARD

Aurora's four-storey-high Atrium is the impressive first sight for passengers on boarding the ship. Passengers enter this room as they board on either Promenade Deck or F Deck, depending on where the ship is berthed.

The Atrium provides stair access between the four entertainment decks, as well as an impressive view of each of the public rooms that overlook the Atrium. Lift access is available at the nearby central stairway.

The Atrium is dominated by a large sculpture by British artist, John Mills. The sculpture, which depicts two figures veiled in water, is entitled *Waterfall* and spans all four decks.

As its name suggests, the sculpture includes a functioning waterfall, which operates except for when the ship is in rough weather. Below the waterfall is an illuminated pool, which contains further water features in the shape of clamshells.

ACCOMMODATION ABOARD

Aurora offers ten main cabin categories, which range from double-storey penthouse suites with a forward-facing view, to more modest, yet still comfortable, inside cabins.

SUITES

In addition to two double-height penthouse suites on B Deck there are also a number of other suites and mini-suites located on both B and C Decks.

Suite accommodation offers a comfortable bedroom, as well as a separate dining area, lounge, balcony, and a spacious bathroom with a spa bath. The larger suites offer a walk-in wardrobe as well as an optional butler service.

The largest and most impressive suites aboard *Aurora* are the Library Suite and Piano Suite. These rooms are located across both A Deck and B Deck and offer a balcony as well as forward-facing windows.

The Library Suite is so named because it has a small library, while the Piano Suite offers a baby grand piano.

Just one deck down, the Canberra Suite and Oriana Suite offer luxury in a single-storey format; with the Oriana Suite providing an optional third and fourth berth; perfect for families.

Did you know ?

Aurora was named by HRH *The Princess Royal* (Princess Anne).

BALCONY CABINS

Aurora offers a range of balcony cabins designed to suit a range of budgets. These vary from the large deluxe balcony cabins on B Deck, to standard balcony rooms on Lido, A, B and C Decks.

The balcony cabins provide a bedroom with large twin beds convertible to a queen, a curtained-off seating area with couch and, of course, a balcony.

Tea and coffee making facilities are available, as well as a TV, a radio and a writing desk; while an in-room iron, ironing board and trouser press reduce the need to visit the communal laundry.

LETTERS AND NUMBERS

One of the quirks of *Aurora* is that passenger decks are both named and numbered. For example, F Deck is home to cabins in the 5-thousand series. This means your room on F Deck is referred to as F123 but when making telephone calls to that cabin you must dial 5123. This can take a bit of getting used to for new *Aurora* travellers.

OUTSIDE CABINS

Outside cabins offer travellers a view and are positioned across six decks. Bright and airy thanks to the large window, these cabins provide a bedroom, writing desk, vanity mirror and compact yet functional en suite bathroom.

As with all cabin categories, outside cabins come with a twice daily cleaning and turn down service.

The outside grade offers single occupancy rooms, with four forward-facing cabins located on A and C Decks. This consideration not only delights single travellers but also allows for a unique view over the bow of the ship.

INSIDE CABINS

Located on each of the accommodation decks are inside cabins. As the name suggests, these cabins have no balcony or window and are both the smallest and most affordable way to travel aboard *Aurora*.

Regardless of your cabin grade, each evening you will find your bed turned down with a P&O branded chocolate and the next day's Horizon daily programme awaiting you.

INSIDE OUTSIDE

By nature of the inside cabins having no windows, you may think all of these cabins are restricted to areas of the ship away from the sides of the ship. Not so! Aboard *Aurora* cabin D102 and D103 are among a row of outside cabins; however, the ship's hull design means these rooms cannot offer a window and as such are sold as inside grade cabins.

RESTAURANTS ABOARD

Aurora offers a range of dining options from traditional ocean liner style dining to casual eateries and grills.

There are two formal dining rooms aboard; one which provides a set table service and the other a walk-in service.

If you prefer a less structured experience, the ship's buffet is the place for you; while on deck burgers, fries and ready-made salads are offered as quick meals.

For passengers looking to experience something special aboard *Aurora*, the extra tariff restaurants provide tantalising meal options that are sure to satisfy your cravings.

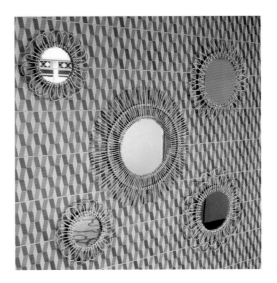

Restaurant Profile

Name	Location
Alexandria Restaurant	E Deck
Medina Restaurant	E Deck
Horizon Restaurant	Lido Deck
Lido Café	Lido Deck
Sindhu	D Deck
The Glass House	D Deck
The Beach House	Lido Deck

ALEXANDRIA RESTAURANT

Taking its name from the Egyptian port that once formed the backbone of the P&O Suez service, the Alexandria restaurant dominates the aft end of E Deck.

Situated off the aft stairway, it is separated from the rest of the deck by the galley; meaning guests without a reservation at this venue might not stumble upon it.

The restaurant is accessible via stairs that open into a vast room, which by day is flooded with natural light. Large windows on the port and starboard sides are

complemented by an aft-facing vista allowing passengers the opportunity to view the ship's wake while enjoying their meal.

Dinner reservations are required as the restaurant operates 'set seating' with guests dining with the same group of people each evening. Tables are available for groups of two to eight, with the same waiters serving at the table each night, allowing for a more traditional dining experience.

Did you know ?

Until the opening of the Suez Canal in 1869, passengers travelling on P&O ships from England to India and beyond would disembark in Alexandria and take the Overland Route to Suez. The Overland Route involved travel by canal boat, river steamer and a carriage ride, and took 60 hours, including rest time.

MEDINA RESTAURANT

The Medina Restaurant is located amidships on E Deck. Though the restaurant is technically accessible from both Prom Deck and E Deck, it is often only operating with the E Deck entry.

The Medina Restaurant takes its name from the 1911 P&O liner. The restaurant is decorated in a Moorish theme, taking inspiration from a style linked to the Iberian Peninsula region, which is the area where the company first operated.

Passengers are seated at tables of two to eight, with electronic calling beacons handed out when the restaurant is full. Serving breakfast, lunch and dinner, the Medina Restaurant is a popular venue for those who enjoy the formalities of a meal with waiter service, but who like to meet new people at dinner each night.

Did you know ?

In 1911 the P&O liner *Medina* was chartered for use as a royal yacht to transport King George V and Queen Mary to the Durbar at Delhi, India. HMS *Medina* departed Portsmouth with the royal couple aboard on 11 November 1911.

HORIZON RESTAURANT

Did you know?

The ship's daily newsletter is also called Horizon.

Buffets are always very popular on cruise ships thanks to the wide selection of food and their casual atmosphere. Add to this, sweeping views from the floor-to-ceiling windows, comfortable furniture and a beach-like ambiance and you've got the Horizon Restaurant aboard *Aurora*.

Located on Lido Deck, seating is divided into different zones that run along the port and starboard sides of the room.

A central buffet offers a number of individual stations, providing hot meals, cold meals and cook-to-order options, popular at breakfast allowing passengers to have their eggs cooked just the way they like them.

Light woods, blue fabric accents and an artistic take on ship schematics complete the restaurant to create a popular venue.

Did you know?

There is a self-service wine bar in the Horizon Restaurant. The Enomatic system allows passengers to swipe their cruise card to purchase a selection of wines by the glass.

LIDO CAFÉ

For those wishing to grab a quick bite to eat whilst enjoying the on-deck areas, the Lido Café is the place to go. Situated on Lido Deck between the Crystal and Riviera Pools, the Lido Café is an informal eatery with a 'grab-and-go' service.

Burgers, hot dogs, chicken rolls and chips are available from the hot grill, while salads, fruit, vegetables and desserts are provided from a series of self-service refrigerators.

Coffee lovers will appreciate the speciality Costa Coffee available here, while those with a sweet tooth will revel at the nearby ice cream shop where speciality ice cream is available for an extra decadent indulgence.

Did you know ?

Lido is an Italian word for beach.

SINDHU

The Sindhu Restaurant was created by multi-Michelin star winning celebrity chef Atul Kochhar, and is located on the starboard side of D Deck.

The Sindhu Restaurant serves Indian cuisine. Kochhar is regularly aboard *Aurora* to train and mentor new chefs who follow his specific recipes aboard the ship.

The restaurant's current décor was introduced during *Aurora*'s last refit and is vibrant in its design. Tiled floors with a star-shaped mosaic are situated beneath an elegant chandelier. The entry is flanked by a selection of fine wine in glass-fronted shelving; while large windows bathe the space in natural light.

With a dedicated team of waiters, sommeliers and chefs, Sindhu is well suited to live up to its promise of an extra special dining experience at sea, and is well worth the additional tariff.

THE GLASS HOUSE

Inspired by celebrity wine expert Olly Smith, the Glass House is a split-level alternative dining venue situated mid-aft on D Deck.

Accessible from D Deck, it can also be entered via a spiral staircase from Prom Deck. The Prom Deck stairwell is crowned by a huge circular chandelier.

The Glass House is decorated in a bright and clean style with plush furniture interspersed with thin and elegant tables and chairs; a grand circular balustrade, panelled shutters and light-coloured walls.

An extra tariff restaurant, the Glass House experience sees menu choices paired with appropriate wines to create a both tasty and educational experience.

THE BEACH HOUSE

Situated at the aft end of the Horizon Restaurant, The Beach House is an understated extra tariff dining option.

Decorated in the same theme as Horizon, it is transformed at night into a casual yet elegant eatery with set tables, mood lighting and a specialised family-friendly grill menu.

On warm weather cruises, the restaurant spills out onto the aft deck to allow for a pleasant meal in an open-air setting.

Did you know ?

Aurora was built at Meyer Werft shipyard in Germany.

BARS & LOUNGES

For many people, a cruise holiday is an opportunity to relax, unwind and be looked after in a way seldom achievable at home. *Aurora* is well suited to allowing passengers an opportunity to slow down and enjoy life, with a range of elegant bars and lounges to discover.

Whether you're looking for a quiet nook to curl up with a good book, a warm and sunny open-air venue to enjoy a romantic cocktail with a loved one, or prefer a vibrant and engaging gathering with friends in one of the many lounges, you'll find *Aurora* offers it all.

WHAT ENTERTAINMENT?

When P&O first started operating services around the world, passenger entertainment and amenities were markedly different to those enjoyed aboard *Aurora*.

As recently as the 1950s, passengers used to form their own social committees on the first day at sea with the committee arranging much of the onboard entertainment. When it came to activities, such as quizzes and bingo, the committee would even buy the prizes in the various ports the ship visited!

Did you know ?

Aurora has two rudders.

Bars & Lounges Profile

Name	Location
The Crow's Nest	Sun Deck
Uganda Room	Sun Deck
Riviera Bar	Lido Deck
Crystal Bar	Lido Deck
Pennant Bar	Lido Deck
Raffles Court & Bar	D Deck
Vanderbilt's	D Deck
Anderson's	Prom Deck
Charlie's	Prom Deck
Masquerade	Prom Deck
Champions Bar & Casino	Prom Deck
Carmen's	Prom Deck

THE CROW'S NEST

The Crow's Nest takes its name from the lookout platform that once adorned the masts of all passenger liners. First established on P&O's much-loved *Canberra*; it has become a signature room aboard the P&O Cruises fleet.

Set high atop the ship on Sun Deck, The Crow's Nest offers uninterrupted views over the bow, port and starboard sides of the ship, with large floor-to-ceiling windows being the most noticeable feature of the space.

It is a popular venue both day and night, with pianists and vocalists performing during the evening; while during the day it is a quiet and relaxing lounge where drinks are served by the friendly and attentive wait staff.

Due to its views, this is a popular location for passengers to watch the sail away as well as transits of the world's great waterways such as the Suez and Panama Canals – but be quick, as the only forward-facing public room aboard the ship fills up quickly!

UGANDA ROOM

The Uganda Room takes its name from the passenger ship *Uganda*, which entered service with P&O in 1971. The Uganda Room is a function room, and a quiet and relaxing lounge when not being used for functions.

Situated just aft of The Crow's Nest, it is located on the starboard side of Sun Deck with direct access and also has an entrance from The Crow's Nest.

This venue plays host to a variety of events, including weddings, religious services, art classes, health and wellness seminars and small lectures as part of the ship's enrichment programme.

On display here is a large model of the ship *Uganda*, resplendent with a white hull and unconventional black and white funnel.

Visitors to this room can be forgiven for not immediately noticing the model due to large floor-to-ceiling windows, which offer excellent views of the various cruising destinations *Aurora* visits.

Did you know ?

SS *Uganda* was requisitioned for use as a hospital ship during the Falklands War. She was operated with the call sign 'Mother Hen'.

RIVIERA BAR

The Riviera Bar is located on Lido Deck and overlooks the Riviera Pool on A Deck. An open-air bar, it is protected by awnings that offer shade and sun-protection to people looking to enjoy a casual drink.

Patrons can choose to take their drink to one of the nearby deck chairs laid out in a split-level arrangement, surrounding the Riviera Pool. Other seating options include bar stools that face aft, with a view of the ship's funnel.

Did you know ?

Aurora is wider than the narrowest parts of the Suez Canal were when it first opened.

CRYSTAL BAR

Located just forward of the Crystal Pool on the starboard side is the Crystal Bar.

As the name suggests, it is designed to service the Crystal Pool area as well as the indoor/outdoor deck under *Aurora*'s retractable Skydome Glass Roof.

Taking the form of a curved bar façade under a tall awning, the bar itself is decorated in brown hues complete with wooden-topped bar stools. Drinks are available for order at the bar, or via roaming bar staff attending those enjoying the deck chairs placed nearby.

During world cruises, the Crystal Bar and surrounding areas are sometimes transformed into popup evening dinner venues, specialising in foods of the respective destinations.

Popular examples include the Aussie barbecue hosted when the ship calls at Sydney, as well as a South African braai during calls at Cape Town.

Did you know ?

The first *Aurora* was an Orient Line ship. Orient Line was absorbed into P&O in 1961.

The Crystal Bar overlooks the
Crystal Pool and Spas.
Courtesy Andrew Sassoli-Walker.

PENNANT BAR

Enjoying unparalleled views over the aft of *Aurora*, the Pennant Bar is a firm favourite with passengers on sunny summer cruises.

The name of this outdoor bar was inspired by the P&O house pennant that has been flown aboard the company's ships since the earliest days of the line's formation.

With a casual atmosphere, this open-air bar has shade sails to offer patrons protection from the sun. The oval-shaped bar area serves a range of alcoholic and non-alcoholic drinks, as well as snacks and canapés.

Did you know ?

Aurora was the largest P&O Cruises ship when she entered service in 2000.

Above: Courtesy Andrew Sassoli-Walker.

Did you know ?

Aurora was the first P&O Cruises ship to be repainted in the new company livery.

RAFFLES BAR & COURT

One of the most popular areas aboard *Aurora* is the Raffles Bar. Situated on D Deck, it hugs the Atrium, offering passengers an opportunity to enjoy a drink while the quiet sounds of the ship's waterfall create a peaceful environment.

Coffee is the most popular drink here, with a Costa Coffee bar. This barista bar serves drinks all day long and well into the night. While most people come to the café knowing what kind of hot beverage they want, the café's cake selection will prove more difficult, as the shipboard chefs dazzle patrons with an array of choices ranging from lavish cupcake designs to Swedish Princess Cake.

There is ample seating, courtesy of the adjoining Raffles Court, which offers tables for two, four and six with comfy chairs and couches.

VANDERBILT'S

If you fancy a game of cards or want to learn how to play popular games such as Bridge, head to Vanderbilt's.

This cosy location is found amidships on D Deck and is an L-shape allowing access from both the forward and aft ends of the room.

While it is primarily the ship's card room, it also acts as a meeting place for small gatherings, interest groups and topical lectures.

Little known to many passengers is the boardroom located next to Vanderbilt's. This relatively private room consists of a 14-seat board table and can be used for those guests who are working at sea. In reality, it is more often used by *Aurora*'s senior crew for staff meetings.

TERRACE BAR

Located on the aft end of D Deck, the Terrace Bar is named for the area of the ship that it occupies and refers to the ship's terraced stern. Servicing the area surrounding the Terrace Pool, the Terrace Bar is an open air location, popular on sunny days.

Roaming wait staff provide service direct to your sunbathing location, or passengers can choose to sit at the bar.

Courtesy Andrew Sassoli-Walker.

Courtesy Patricia Dempsey.

ANDERSON'S

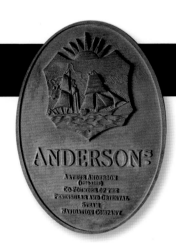

Quiet and relaxed, Anderson's evokes the golden age of the ocean liner. Named after one of P&O's founders, Arthur Anderson, this lounge is finished in a traditional style, with numerous nods to P&O's long history.

The room includes a mock-fireplace, which resembles the real wood-burning open fires common on the old ocean liners. In addition, model ships and paintings of the P&O fleet give the room a proud sense of history.

Did you know ?

Arthur Anderson enlisted in the Royal Navy at the age of 16 and fought in the Napoleonic Wars.

In the main entry a large portrait of Arthur Anderson himself makes the link between *Aurora* and the founder of P&O, while in the centre of the room a large faux wood clad bar completes the space and serves drinks from early afternoon into the wee hours of the morning.

CHARLIE'S

Some of the most delightful parts about *Aurora* are the small, intimate bars and lounges found scattered about the ship. Catering to a wide range of passengers, they are especially welcome during long-duration voyages.

Utilising what might have otherwise been wasted space, these bars and lounges add a unique atmosphere to the ship and create a sense of wonder as new venues are discovered during the voyage.

Charlie's is one such bar. Situated in a nook between the Mayfair Court shops and Anderson's, Charlie's is a wine bar. It doubles as a quiet lounge area and is popular with passengers wishing to relax in a quiet corner with a good book.

A baby grand piano is Charlie's most notable feature, with pianists entertaining guests during evening hours, as well as occasional recitals during the day.

With a port-side view overlooking the promenade deck, and a starboard-side vista of the main Atrium, Charlie's is a venue that will stick in the mind of anyone who takes the time to relax here.

Did you know ?

In 2001, *Aurora* went to the aid of the Cambodian vessel *Pamela Dream*.

MASQUERADE

Set amidships on Prom Deck and accessed by following a curved glass wall off the main promenade, Masquerade is one of *Aurora*'s nightclubs.

Masquerade has an industrial-style design, with a modern feel. The finishes are polished metals, glass and chrome, and brightly coloured chairs and carpets. The wall panels feature blue outlines of costumed figures.

A split-level room, its central focus is a round dance floor and petite, raised stage, which allows late night dancing to a live band.

CHAMPIONS BAR & CASINO ⟿

For much of P&O's history, the line's main purpose was to connect the United Kingdom with its overseas dominions, Commonwealth countries and territories.

One unavoidable element of this service was the intense sporting rivalry that existed between various nations – often evident during long-duration P&O voyages.

Ships such as *Canberra* and the original *Oriana* payed tribute to this rivalry by including a sports bar aboard, while the 'new' *Oriana* of 1995 took this concept one step further with the expansive sports bar called Champions.

So popular was Champions aboard *Oriana* that it was included aboard *Aurora*. Here, the space is decorated with sporting memorabilia with a particular focus

Did you know ?

Aurora's maiden voyage was cancelled after the first day at sea due to technical issues with the ship's engines.

on cricket. In fact, a collection of cricket bats and balls, as well as other sporting apparel, can be found prominently displayed around the room.

Live sporting events are broadcast here via satellite and displayed on large flat-panel TV screens, while drinks available from the bar include draught beer and an international selection of wines and spirits.

The ship's Casino is located within Champions where passengers can try their luck at a variety of table games or slot machines.

CARMEN'S 🌀

A multi-purpose venue at the aft end of Prom Deck, Carmen's can't be missed thanks to the bold red-walled entry statement complete with statues of dancers.

As hinted by the artwork, Carmen's is a dance venue, with a large wooden dance floor, stage and modern sound and light setup. It is also *Aurora*'s second show lounge.

Smaller than the Curzon Theatre, Carmen's feels like an intimate venue with a welcoming and cosy feel. Yet in reality it is large

Did you know ?

Aurora's first successful cruise occurred in May 2000. The voyage was to the Canary Islands.

enough to host large-scale events from dance lessons to bingo and everything in between.

At night, the venue comes into its own, with live music creating a party atmosphere. Despite *Aurora* having a nightclub in Masquerade, Carmen's is equally popular for late night dancing, with the music often going until the early hours of the morning.

PUBLIC AREAS

While strictly built for cruising, *Aurora*'s design offers a timeless elegance that is reminiscent of the great ocean liners of yesteryear. This design is carried over to her various public spaces, where a variety of offerings from a library to a cinema, show lounges to the spa, ensure the ship appeals to a wide audience.

Did you know ?

Aurora's call sign is ZCDW9.

Those who fancy a quiet read with a view of the ocean, can head to the ship's Library, which is staffed by a professional librarian.

Passengers who prefer to take in the latest blockbuster movie will be delighted to find The Playhouse, *Aurora*'s full-sized dedicated cinema, an inclusion rarely found on modern-day cruise ships.

Or for those of a sportier persuasion, the ship's gym offers a mix of cardio equipment, weights and fitness classes.

Public Areas Profile

Name	Location
Library	Sun Deck
Oasis Spa & Salon	Lido Deck
Weights and Measures Fitness Room	A Deck
Photo Gallery	D Deck
The Playhouse	D Deck
The Reef (Splashers, Scubas, Surfers, h2o)	D Deck
Curzon Theatre	Prom Deck
Mayfair Court	Prom Deck
Explorers (Tour Sale office)	E Deck
Piccadilly	E Deck
Emporium	E Deck
Palm Court	F Deck
Future Cruise Sales & Loyalty	F Deck
Laundrettes	Various Decks

Did you know ?

Aurora's official number is 9169524.

LIBRARY

In days gone by, reading a good book on a deck chair was one of the most popular pastimes for passengers, and even in today's modern world it is still one of life's little joys.

To satisfy this desire, *Aurora* has her own shipboard library. Managed by a specialist team of shipboard librarians, the Library is found on Sun Deck, just aft of The Crow's Nest. It is stocked with a wide range of fiction and non-fiction books, covering a range of genres from romance and thriller, to history and biographies.

The Library is also home to *Aurora*'s computer centre. Here, a number of computers can be accessed allowing travellers to surf the web and write emails. Access to the Internet is at an additional cost and can be arranged by buying an Internet package. The ship is also fully Wi-Fi enabled, meaning you can connect your device on the go!

Did you know ?

Aurora was laid down on 15 December 1998.

OASIS SPA & SALON

For many, the definition of luxury and relaxation is a day at the spa. But who has the time? Fortunately, during a cruise holiday, time is on your side, and *Aurora* has a luxury spa and salon to make your dreams a reality.

True to its name, the Oasis Spa & Salon is a tranquil retreat where passengers can relax and luxuriate in quiet, welcoming surroundings. The space is decorated in a calming theme with ocean views to allow those visiting an opportunity to be pampered while connecting with their surroundings.

The spa and salon offers many services including facials, massage, acupuncture, hair treatments, manicures, pedicures and make-up consultations.

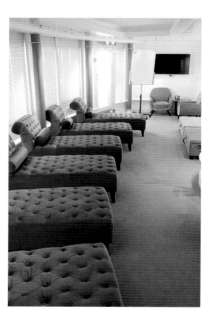

Did you know ?

Aurora was launched on 18 January 2000.

WEIGHTS & MEASURES FITNESS ROOM

Situated on A Deck and accessible from the Oasis Spa & Salon on Lido Deck, is the Weights and Measures Fitness Room.

Aurora's passenger gym, the space benefits from large windows, which offer a view out to the cascading waterfall feature, at the aft end of the Riviera Pool.

A central exercise space is the most prominent focal point here, with wooden floors and mirrors typical of an aerobics or yoga studio.

This area is surrounded by an array of cardio and weight-bearing apparatus with equipment updated regularly to ensure the latest fitness trends are available at sea. Popular items include the Concept2 rowing machines, of which *Aurora* has three, as well as treadmills and cross-trainers which are equipped with personal TV screens allowing gym-goers to catch up on the latest news via the ship's satellite television service.

Instructors are on hand to teach visitors how to use the various apparatus, and organised exercise classes are held at times advertised in the ship's daily programme.

PHOTO GALLERY

'Would you like your picture taken?' is something you hear often during a cruise and *Aurora* is no exception.

A team of professional photographers travel with the ship, snapping special moments that range from formal cocktail parties, to dinner, shore tours and sail away.

These images are processed and displayed in the Photo Gallery. Located just aft of The Playhouse, this is a traditional take on shipboard photography with printed images displayed during sea-days for passengers to purchase.

DVDs about *Aurora* and your journey can be purchased here, while printing services are available for those wishing to have their own photographs printed.

Did you know ?

Aurora cost US$375 million to build.

THE PLAYHOUSE

In days gone by, the inclusion of a cinema was a rare luxury aboard passenger ships. Those that provided such amenities were considered top-class and at the cutting edge of modern trends.

Today, the cinema space on most cruise ships has disappeared, absorbed into the large multi-purpose show lounge. Not so aboard *Aurora*.

The Playhouse cinema seats over 200, offering patrons excellent sight lines and surround sound. It is very popular, with several movie screenings during the day. Decorated in a modern take on art deco, The Playhouse evokes a sense of cosy anticipation and is dressed in warm tones of burgundy, gold and wood.

When not in use as a cinema, the space doubles as a lecture venue, where guest speakers entertain passengers on a range of topics.

THE REEF

If you're travelling with children *Aurora* has ample facilities to keep the kids entertained. Entertainment comes in the way of a series of youth hubs that take their naming inspiration from an ocean theme.

Splashers caters for the youngest travellers. Here, 2- to 4-year-olds can enjoy games and entertainment in a safe and age-friendly environment. Splashers has both indoor and outdoor play areas.

For more mature children, Surfers and Scubas provide entertainment for 5- to 8-year-olds and 9- to 12-year-olds respectively. Here, P&O's 'Reef Rangers' create fun adventures and organise sports games and quieter pursuits.

Finally, h2o is available for 13- to 17-year-olds with movies, games and parties held here.

In addition to the daytime activities *Aurora* also makes allowances for night time. Those travelling with children aged 6 months to 4 years can take advantage of the night nursery. Here children are supervised and can sleep in a quiet and comfortable environment while their parents enjoy a night off. Parents are provided with a pager to allow easy contact should their child require assistance.

CURZON THEATRE

Whether enjoying a daytime enrichment lecture, matinee classical concert or evening production show, the Curzon Theatre is the place for all.

Found at the forward end of Prom Deck, this gently terraced room can seat over 650 passengers in comfortable padded maroon seats.

The room offers excellent sightlines and is decorated with dark-wood panelled walls, rich blue carpeting accented with red details and polished gold lettering on its entry signage.

Did you know ?

Aurora's yard number (build number) was 640.

The stage is located at the forward end and spans 22m, allowing for a variety of productions to be offered during the cruise. A drinks service is provided on some formal nights thanks to the nearby bar at Anderson's.

On the first night of longer voyages entertainment staff invite guest speakers, entertainers and musicians onto the stage to introduce them to passengers, creating a friendly and engaging atmosphere where guests are encouraged to interact with those providing entertainment.

MAYFAIR COURT

Most cruise ships have the nautical equivalent of a general store, where you'll find an array of useful goods, from paperbacks to sea sickness tablets.

Aboard *Aurora*, this store goes by the name Mayfair and is located starboard and aft of the Atrium on Prom Deck.

If the ample complimentary indulgence of sugary delights hasn't satisfied your sweet tooth, Mayfair provides a selection of British chocolates, while also selling more mundane goods such as batteries, medication and sunscreen.

In addition Mayfair offers a wide selection of clothing for men, women and children, as well as P&O and *Aurora* branded items.

EXPLORERS

Aurora's annual cruise schedule takes her to exciting and exotic destinations around the world. The ship is well suited for cruising. Being a mid-sized vessel she can access many of the world's favourite destinations as well as transit both the Suez and Panama Canals.

For those passengers wishing to discover new cruise destinations, a shore excursion is a good first step. Organised by a professional onboard team, the tours are sold from the Explorers cruise sales desk on E Deck.

Comfortable seating, friendly staff and an array of booklets and collateral helps eager travellers identify and choose the tour that best suits them, while having a shipboard-arranged tour comes with the added security of knowing if the bus is late, the ship will wait!

PICCADILLY & EMPORIUM

The most exclusive of *Aurora*'s shops, Piccadilly is found on E Deck, near the Atrium. Exclusive brands are the mainstay of Piccadilly, with designer clothes, jewellery, cosmetics and perfumes on offer.

The duty-free prices as well as the friendly and attentive staff make Piccadilly a popular spot for passengers to treat themselves or pick up a gift for a loved one back home.

E Deck is also home to the Emporium shop which can be found forward of Piccadilly on the starboard side of the ship.

A smaller shop than the others aboard, Emporium offers a range of traditional duty-free items such as alcohol and perfume.

PALM COURT

Like the concierge at a good hotel, the purser's office aboard a highly regarded cruise ship such as *Aurora* is tasked with ensuring passengers have a stress-free and relaxing stay on board.

Aboard *Aurora*, this office is called Palm Court, and is located at the lowest level of the Atrium on F Deck.

A large curved reception desk can be found against the aft end of the space, facing the Atrium staircase. A welcoming atmosphere is created with fresh flowers and the sound of running water thanks to the nearby waterfalls incorporated into the central sculpture featured in the Atrium.

Some notable features of Palm Court include an officer's sword and a portrait of HRH The Princess Royal, who named *Aurora* and is the ship's official godmother.

Did you know ?

Aurora was originally registered in London, UK.

FUTURE CRUISE SALES & LOYALTY ◗◗

They say the best part about the end of a cruise is the chance to start planning the next one. Aboard *Aurora*, you don't need to wait until you get home!

The Peninsular Club is P&O Cruises loyalty programme. Representatives are on hand at the Future Bookings Desk on F Deck to assist in searching for and booking a cruise on any of P&O's British-based ships.

LAUNDRETTES

Despite generous baggage allowances on cruise ships, keeping clothes clean on long-duration voyages can be quite a challenge.

Aboard *Aurora*, it is as simple and easy as possible thanks to not one, but several large, self-service laundrettes located across a number of passenger decks.

In each of these rooms, you'll find washing machines and dryers, as well as irons and ironing boards for individual use. Washing detergent is available in the laundrette while seating is provided for those guests wishing to wait for their washing cycle to finish.

These areas are particularly useful during longer voyages such as the annual World Cruise, where the expense of the ship's paid laundry service could add a considerable bill to your cabin account.

Did you know ?

Today *Aurora* is registered in Hamilton, Bermuda.

GETTING AROUND

There are ten decks aboard *Aurora* for passengers to enjoy, and connecting the various shipboard areas are a number of stairways, corridors and lifts.

Aurora has a relatively simple layout, with three main stairways linking the passenger decks. These are arranged in an orderly fashion, with one forward, one aft and one amidships.

The G Deck medical centre is only accessible from the aft stairway, while F Deck utilises the forward and amidships stairs and lifts.

The various corridors, stairways and alleyways are lined with artworks that add character and create a sense of place, making *Aurora* feel friendly, accessible and luxurious.

ON DECK

Aurora was built as a one-off, unique cruise ship. Taking inspiration from the 1995-built *Oriana*, *Aurora*'s design incorporates a variety of classic ocean liner features, none more noticeable than her open decks.

Unlike many modern cruise ships where outdoor areas are covered in faux wood flooring, the bulk of *Aurora*'s decks are completed in a more traditional teakwood finish; giving the ship an old-fashioned charm despite her relative youth.

Aurora also benefits from an elegant stern design, with her aft decks terraced down from Sun Deck to D Deck. This doesn't just give the ship a very attractive appearance, but also provides ample space for passengers to promenade or gather around wooden tables and chairs for an on-deck drink.

On-Deck Areas Profile

Name	Location
Sports Court	Sun Deck
Crystal Pool	Lido Deck
Riviera Pool	A Deck
Terrace Pool	D Deck
Promenade Deck	Prom Deck
Observation Platforms	Various Decks

SPORTS COURT

For some travellers, the idea of exercising while on a cruise is quite unappealing; for others the thought of fresh air, warm sun and a game of tennis is just what the doctor ordered.

Aurora caters for all levels of sporting enthusiasm, from gentle pursuits in a game of shuffleboard, to a more energetic engagement such as basketball.

The Sports Court is situated on Sun Deck and hosts much of the outdoor sporting activity aboard the ship. Activities include a large tennis court which doubles as a basketball court, golf nets, deck quoits, shuffleboard and a jogging area.

The ship also offers a golf simulator where world-class courses from around the world are available for players of all skill levels to test out.

CRYSTAL POOL

Situated forward of the Horizon Restaurant and protected from the elements by the Skydome Glass Roof, the Crystal Pool is open for business whatever the weather might be outside.

Deck chairs and recliners, as well as tables surround the large pool where drinks are served from the nearby Crystal Bar. Hot tubs are available on a raised platform, while garden beds with palm trees give the space a tropical feel.

During sunny days and warm weather cruising, the Skydome can be opened to allow in some fresh air.

RIVIERA POOL

Situated between Lido Deck and A Deck, just aft of the Riviera Bar you'll find the Riviera Pool. Located in the centre of an elegantly terraced deck arrangement, the Riviera Pool forms the focal point of this popular on-deck location.

Its split-level location allows the Riviera Pool to be observed from multiple levels, including through large windows of the Weights and Measures Fitness Room, which is located aft of the pool on A Deck.

TERRACE POOL

One of the key features of *Aurora* that makes her stand out among most modern cruise ships are her beautifully terraced aft decks. The design offers ample deck space with a view over the stern of the ship.

Right towards the back of D Deck on the lowest level of this terraced affect is the aptly named Terrace Pool. The centrepiece of an engaging activities deck, the pool is the focus and surrounded by a hot tub, children's paddling pool and the nearby Terrace Bar.

At the forward end of this space are indoors-outdoors areas from Splashers and Surfers, which allow children access to the open deck in a safe and controlled environment.

With casual seating and the nearby bar, it is a popular location for catching up with friends, sunbathing and the 'Crossing the Line' ceremony when the ship crosses the Equator.

PROMENADE DECK

The Promenade Deck (or Prom Deck for short) is the fourth lowest passenger deck. A full wrap-around deck, it is sheltered inboard, allowing it to be used in almost every weather condition.

The ship's lifeboats are located here, with sixteen boats suspended above Prom Deck on neatly arranged davits. The design is such that the boats and associated machinery don't restrict or obstruct views from the open deck, though windows of some of the public rooms on D Deck do have lifeboat-restricted views.

The ship's wide wrap-around Promenade is adorned with real teakwood flooring, while the ship's design includes a magnificent terraced aft that allows

for ample viewing spaces towards the back of the ship, connected to Prom Deck via wooden stairs.

The on-deck areas are some of the nicest nautical elements of the ship. White railings with polished wooden tops complement the *Aurora* branded lifebuoys to create a truly timeless feel aboard the ship.

Traditionalists will love the wooden steamer deck chairs on Promenade Deck, as well as wooden tables and chairs set up to allow passengers a pleasant vantage point to enjoy a drink and watch the ocean pass by.

OBSERVATION PLATFORMS ೨⋙

Aurora has several forward-facing observation platforms accessible from discreetly placed doors at the front of A, B and C Decks.

Unpublished on *Aurora*'s deck plans, these areas offer quiet and relaxing spaces for viewing the ship's arrivals and departures from various ports around the world. These observation decks are closed in bad weather or high winds, but prove popular locations during unique cruising experiences such as the transit of the Panama Canal.

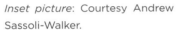

Inset picture: Courtesy Andrew Sassoli-Walker.

WORLD CRUISES

Despite being built to operate as a primarily British-based cruise ship, *Aurora*'s unique design lends itself to long-duration cruising. Her ample open decks, vast outdoor activities spaces, multiple swimming pools and spacious public areas make her a comfortable yet homely way to see the world.

As such, the ship regularly undertakes a World Cruise for P&O Cruises. In this role, *Aurora* has visited many locations around the world and is much loved in

international ports as far from home as Auckland in New Zealand and Sydney in Australia.

During her 2002 World Cruise, *Aurora* sailed across the Great Australian Bight in tandem with the Cunard liner *QE2*. When the two ships arrived in Fremantle, *Aurora* set the record as the largest cruise ship to visit the Australian port at the time.

Aurora's popularity isn't restricted to the Southern Hemisphere. Her speedy yet elegant lines, casual and friendly onboard atmosphere and quintessentially British service means she's a popular choice when visiting Japan, Hong Kong and the United States of America.

Above: Courtesy Andrew Sassoli-Walker. *Below right:* Courtesy Patricia Dempsey.

THE PROFILE

With the success of the 1995-built *Oriana*, P&O decided to construct a running mate to operate in the growing British cruise market. This ship became *Aurora*.

Unique in her design, *Aurora* has a pleasing blend of *Oriana*'s most successful elements, with clear influences from the highly successful Princess ships

Above: Aurora at night. Courtesy Andrew Sassoli-Walker.
Right: *Aurora* as seen from one of her tenders in Sydney Harbour, 2016.

that had been designed and introduced during P&O's connection with the American-centric line.

Aurora's profile is bold and modern, yet it evokes a sense of elegance and grace more often associated with the bygone era of the ocean liner.

Her sharp bow, gracefully streamlined forward profile and elegant terraced aft decks give the ship the appearance of a large and elegant ocean-going yacht.

The ship sports a coordinated superstructure, with neatly arranged balconies and windows and an inboard lifeboat deck which takes inspiration from both *Oriana* and *Canberra*.

Her neat profile, ample deck space and tidy on-deck arrangements mean that she appears clean and smart, while remaining modern even during her second decade of service.

Left: *Aurora* at anchor showing off her Union Flag livery.
Right top: *Aurora*'s terraced aft decks.
Right bottom: View from the tender in Sydney Harbour.

THE MAST

Although *Aurora* and *Oriana* are considered sister ships and from a distance share a family resemblance, there are many areas aboard *Aurora* that differ from her elder sister. The mast is one such area, with a completely different design to that of *Oriana*.

Aurora's mast takes the form of an inverted U-shape with twin pylons joined at the top by a curved structure.

Atop sits a central pylon which holds navigational lighting, while forward of the larger structure is a smaller adjoined mast which houses more of the ship's navigational equipment.

Flags are hoisted onto the mast to represent the P&O brand, *Aurora*'s port of registry (Hamilton, Bermuda) as well as the nation the ship is visiting. Further flags can be shown on the mast as well as signals to indicate the ship is at anchor.

Did you know ?

Although registered in Bermuda, which is British territory, *Aurora* still flies the red ensign.

THE FUNNEL

Today painted in a dark blue livery with the golden P&O logo embellished on its side, the ship's funnel wore the traditional buff-colour for much of *Aurora*'s early career. Set around two thirds aft, the funnel's tallest point sits 61.9m above the ship's keel.

Its design was inspired by the funnel aboard *Oriana*, which itself was modelled to pay homage to the elegant twin funnels of P&O's famed *Canberra*. As such, the design has a distinctive twin-uptake aspect to it, while being more stylised and streamlined than that aboard *Oriana*.

Crew can access the funnel casing from G Deck with a stairway that can be climbed all the way to its top – this makes it the tallest stairway aboard the ship.

Did you know ?

Aurora's funnel was the first in the P&O Cruises fleet to be painted blue, which forms part of the line's new livery introduced in 2014.

CREW ONLY  Behind the Scenes

A ship the size of *Aurora* requires a large number of highly skilled and dedicated people not only to ensure the ship is maintained and running smoothly but to serve over 1,870 passengers.

850 people are tasked with *Aurora*'s upkeep – under the command of the ship's captain. Roles vary from senior officers and deck crew to those operating front of house roles such as guest services, shopkeepers and entertainment staff.

However it's the unnoticed army of people that are key to ensuring *Aurora* runs smoothly. These people work deep inside the ship, maintaining the ship's engines, plumbing, air-conditioning, stores and refrigerators, and even managing the waste and recycling plant.

During the voyage, passengers will catch barely a glimpse of these critical crewmembers – who can sometimes be seen performing minor maintenance tasks around the ship.

On port-days as the ship sits alongside, groups of painters will often be spotted touching up the hull to ensure *Aurora* presents as clean, crisp and fresh for the all-important passenger photographs!

Above: Lifeboat davit machinery aboard Aurora.
Right: A yellow emergency telephone.

THE BRIDGE

Set at the forward end of Lido Deck with a view over the bow is *Aurora*'s Bridge. Fully enclosed, it spans the full width of the ship and incorporates both the Bridge proper and two Bridge wings which extend over the port and starboard sides.

Unlike ships of old, the Bridge aboard *Aurora* is spacious and airy. With walls completed in a light wood veneer, the dominant colour in this space is blue, used on both consoles and carpets.

In the centre of the Bridge, a console holds *Aurora*'s surprisingly small wheel which controls the ship's twin rudders; although in reality she is often steered electronically via a pre-determined course set into the ship's navigation computers.

Consoles also hold vital navigation information including radar, electronic charts, telegraphs to control speed and direction as well as controls for the ship's thrusters.

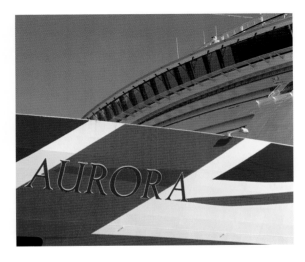

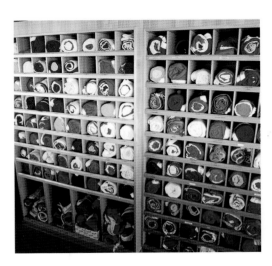

Did you know ?

Aurora was the last passenger ship built for the Peninsular & Oriental Steam Navigation Company before P&O Cruises was sold to the Carnival Corporation.

The steering, thrusters and navigation information is duplicated in separate panels on both Bridge wings, allowing the ship to be safely managed while manoeuvring in close quarters. A small glass window on the floor of each wing offers those driving *Aurora* a view down along the ship's side, essential when docking.

Perhaps the most striking and most definitely the least expected feature on the Bridge is Sven; a stag head mounted to the aft wall on the port side. Donated to the ship by P&O's Olden (Norway) port agent Aslak Lefdal, this feature is found on many of P&O Cruises' ships.

Another striking yet more expected feature of the Bridge is a large open shelving system housing the many different flags the ship requires for the various ports she visits around the world.

AURORA TECHNICAL INFORMATION

Tonnage:	76,152 gross tons
Length:	270m
Width:	32.2m
Draft:	25.9m
Passenger Decks:	10
Main Engines:	Four MAN B&W 48/60 Vee 14 diesel electric engines. Each engine is connected to an alternator producing around 14 megawatts
Speed:	24 knots
Propellers:	Two fixed pitch propellers
Rudders:	Two. One fitted behind each propeller with a 45-degree turning angle
Bow Thrusters:	3 producing 6120HP
Stern Thrusters:	1 producing 2040HP
Stabilisers:	2 Fincantieri design weighing 190 tons each

MASTER'S PERSPECTIVE

Captain Wesley Dunlop

Captain Wesley Dunlop went to sea in 1998, two years before *Aurora* entered service. Joining P&O Cruises in 2016, he has become a well-known and much-loved figure aboard Aurora. Captain Dunlop shared his perspective in March 2017.

Captain Dunlop explains his career, and how he became *Aurora*'s master:

I commenced my seagoing career back in 1998. I was awarded a cadetship with a company called Sun Cruises, they were part of the British travel operator Airtours. They operated four small cruise ships for the UK market, mainly based in the Mediterranean in summer and the Caribbean in winter.

I qualified as Officer of the Watch (OOW) in 2002 and continued to climb the ranks, completing my Chief Officer's licence in 2004 and on my return to sea was lucky enough to be promoted to Chief Officer.

After the end of Sun Cruises in 2004 I was offered various positions but opted to work for Saga, another small British cruise line. I completed my Master's licence in 2006 and was fortunate enough to gain promotion to Staff Captain on the *Saga Rose* (ex *Sagafjord*) in 2007.

In 2010 I took a short break from the cruise industry and worked for Irish Ferries as trainee Master on the *Ulysses* running between Dublin and Holyhead. However, I was soon lured back to cruise ships when offered a full-time position as Master with *Saga* and took command of the *Saga Pearl II* in April 2011 at the age of just 30 (making me I believe the youngest ever cruise ship Master), from there I also commanded the *Saga Ruby* (ex *Vistafjord* and last ever British-built passenger ship), the *Quest for Adventure* and the *Saga Sapphire*.

The highlight of my career, however, came in early 2016 when I was offered the chance to interview for Carnival UK and P&O Cruises. I successfully completed the process and was delighted to be appointed as Master onboard *Aurora*, a duty that I am absolutely relishing!

Captain Dunlop has extensive experience on older tonnage such as the *Saga Rose* and *Saga Ruby*. However, *Aurora* is a modern vessel entering service in 2000...
The layout and systems on board *Aurora* are certainly far more modern than I was used to! The Bridge is the perfect example. However, the Carnival Corporation has a fantastic training and simulator facility in Almere (Netherlands) and it was a requirement that I completed the numerous training courses there prior to taking command.

I won't lie, it was a steep learning curve! Nevertheless it has been worth every minute and it makes a refreshing change to be surrounded by such technology.

That being said, 'cutting my teeth' in the operation of older vessels has proved most useful to me throughout my career, and it is excellent to have had the opportunity to experience both old and new.

With that in mind, Captain Dunlop explains the technical aspects of *Aurora*, such as what machinery the ship uses and how this impacts on operating the vessel:
Aurora is powered and propelled by four diesel generators (14V 48/60) with a total power output of 13,650kW.

She has two inward turning fixed pitch propellers, two spade rudders, three bow thrusters (total 6120HP) and one stern thruster (2040HP).

This makes her a remarkably powerful ship for her size, and certainly aids manoeuvring her in and out of port in difficult conditions.

These days *Aurora* is considered a mid-sized ship, yet at over 76,000 gross tons she is actually quite large. Captain Dunlop explains what it is like to command a ship of this size:

I believe *Aurora* is a perfect sized vessel (not that I'm biased, of course!). She is by far and away the biggest vessel I have ever commanded, but in this modern age she is considered mid-sized.

I've found *Aurora* large enough to be spacious, yet small enough to be intimate. I take pride that as I walk around the ship I can bump into people who I have already met several times throughout the cruise, a rarity in this day and age.

I think it's the size of the ship that really helps to create that welcoming and friendly atmosphere, and it's just one of the many reasons why so many passengers (and crew) love this ship.

My favourite areas on this ship have to be the open decks at the aft end of the ship; the lines are so classic and always make *Aurora* stand out in whichever port we visit.

I also love the main Atrium area, with the flowing statue... and also the Bridge is without a doubt the best office I've ever had!

A Day in the Life of

CAPTAIN DUNLOP

As Master I have overall responsibility for the safe navigation of the ship together with the safety of the passengers, crew and the ship herself.

I also have to have a complete overview of every operation that goes on onboard, although I am a trained deck officer I am responsible for ensuring the other departments (Hotel and Technical etc.) are also meeting the required standards.

Obviously I can't do that all myself, which is why I'm ably assisted by the other members of the Ship's Senior Management Team, namely the Deputy Captain, Chief Engineer, Hotel General Manager and Human Resources Manager.

The one thing I love about my job is that no two days are the same! However, an average day may run something like this:

Courtesy Captain Dunlop.

0530: Arrive on the Bridge and have my first morning coffee! I always like to be on the Bridge 45 minutes before the pilot arrives so I can familiarise myself with the current navigational situation, expected weather and also complete the required checklists with the officers on the Bridge.

0615: Pilot arrives on Bridge and we complete all the formalities of the Master/Pilot exchange. With all the officers on the Bridge we hold a team briefing to discuss the arrival manoeuvre and everyone has the opportunity to raise any questions they may have. All paperwork/checklists are then completed and once this is done we will make our approaches into the port.

0730: Having safely moored the ship alongside I will grab breakfast before heading down to the gangway to see the passengers safely

ashore on their tours. This is a great way of being able to interact with the guests and see several hundred people in a relatively short space of time.

0900–1200: My morning will then be spent catching up on emails, with inspections of the ship and any departmental meetings.

1300–1700: After lunch I will again attend to any paperwork I have together with making a full walk of the ship, I generally like to do this at least twice as it gives me the opportunity to speak with both passengers and crew alike – I genuinely believe as Master it is important to make yourself as visible and approachable as possible.

1700–1800: Departure on the Bridge. Very often if I have completed the arrival manoeuvre I will encourage the Deputy Captain or another officer to complete the departure manoeuvre whilst I fulfil their role; this offers a great learning opportunity for the aspiring Masters in the team.

1900: Following dinner I will then do a final check of the emails in my office and make a last walk of the ship before reporting to the Bridge to write my night orders for the team. Then it's a case of a cup of cocoa and beddy-byes!

BIBLIOGRAPHY

Books:

Poole, S. and Sassoli-Walker, A. (2012), *Oriana & Aurora: Taking UK Cruising into a New Millenium*, Stroud, Amberley Publishing.

Henderson, R., Cremer, D., Cross, R. and Frame, C. (2015), *A Photographic History of P&O Cruises*, Stroud, The History Press.

Company Correspondence:

Various P&O Cruises correspondence relating to technical specifications of *Aurora*.

Personal Conversations:

Captain Wesley Dunlop – P&O Captain, Master of *Aurora*

Michael Mullane – P&O Entertainment Manager, *Aurora*

Jenny Hadley – P&O Public Relations

Anna Goddard & Alice Banet – P&O Entertainment

Andrew Sassoli-Walker – Author

Patricia Dempsey – Shipping Writer / Enthusiast

Websites:

P&O Cruises – www.pocruises.co.uk

Beyond Ships – www.beyondships.com

Chris Frame's website – www.chrisframe.com.au

Aurora in 2007 in her original livery. Courtesy Patricia Dempsey.